*To Camden
Be yourself!*

If I Look Like You

Dawn Brotherton

Dawn Brotherton

Illustrated by Chad Thompson

Published by Blue Dragon Publishing, LLC

Williamsburg, VA

https://BlueDragonPublishing.com

Copyright © 2022 by Dawn Brotherton

Illustrated by Chad Thompson

ISBN: 978-1-939696-89-2 (hardback)

Library of Congress Control Number: 2022931429

All rights reserved.

Printed in China.

26 25 24 23 22   1 2 3 4 5 6 7

"Momma, I look like you. Does that mean I'll be a **welder** when I grow up?"

"You can be anything you want to be," says Scout's mother.

"Anything?" Scout says. "Where should I explore to learn more?"

"If I look like you, I can be an **artist**," Scout says.

"You don't have to look like me," says the artist.

"Do you like to be creative? Painting peaceful places is my pleasure," the artist says. "I reach new heights by painting different scenes."

Scout studies the artwork. "I love making pictures, but before I practice, I need to shop for supplies."

"If I look like you, I can be a **shop owner**," Scout says.

"You don't have to look like me," says the shop owner.

"Do you put your toys away neatly when you're done playing to make them easier to find? It's more satisfying than honey when shoppers successfully find something in my store."

Scout hands him a box. "I like helping my friends find what they're looking for."

She sees someone outside the door. "Who's that flying down the street?"

"If I look like you, I can be a **postal worker**," Scout says.

"You don't have to look like me," says the postal worker. "Do you like being out in all kinds of weather? My spirit soars when I visit customers. I have to be dependable and deliver the mail, no matter what."

Scout follows her down the street. "You can count on me, and I like playing in the rain. You probably deliver to many of the places I go."

"If I look like you, I can be a **dentist**," Scout says.

"You don't have to look like me," says the dentist.

"Do you like looking at a beautiful smile? Helping others keep their teeth and gums healthy is something I can sink my choppers into! I repair patient's teeth when they are painful."

Scout considers the question. "I like getting others to smile, *and* I brush every day. Maybe I could be a dentist."

"Hmmm, thinking about my teeth makes me hungry."

"If I look like you, I can be a **farmer**," Scout says.

"You don't have to look like me," says the farmer.

"Do you like to work in the dirt? It's magical to plant my favorite produce and watch it grow."

"If I look like you, I can be a chef," Scout says.

"You don't have to look like me," says the chef. "Do you like helping in the kitchen? Making dishes from scratch that delight my diners is almost as refreshing as a cool dip in the pool."

Scout smells the delicious food. "I like helping with dinner, and I could learn to make new meals. First, I will make a treat for my teacher."

"If I look like you, I can be a **teacher**," Scout says.

"You don't have to look like me," says the teacher.

"Do you like to teach others what you know? Watching students light up as they learn makes me leap with joy."

Scout laughs. "I taught my brother to ride a skateboard. It was fun. Maybe I could use a computer to learn more things."

"If I look like you, I can be a **computer programmer**," Scout says.

"You don't have to look like me," says the programmer.

"Do you like puzzles? Programming can be like playing a game that makes work easier or more fun. I can happily spend all day pecking at the keyboard to get things just right."

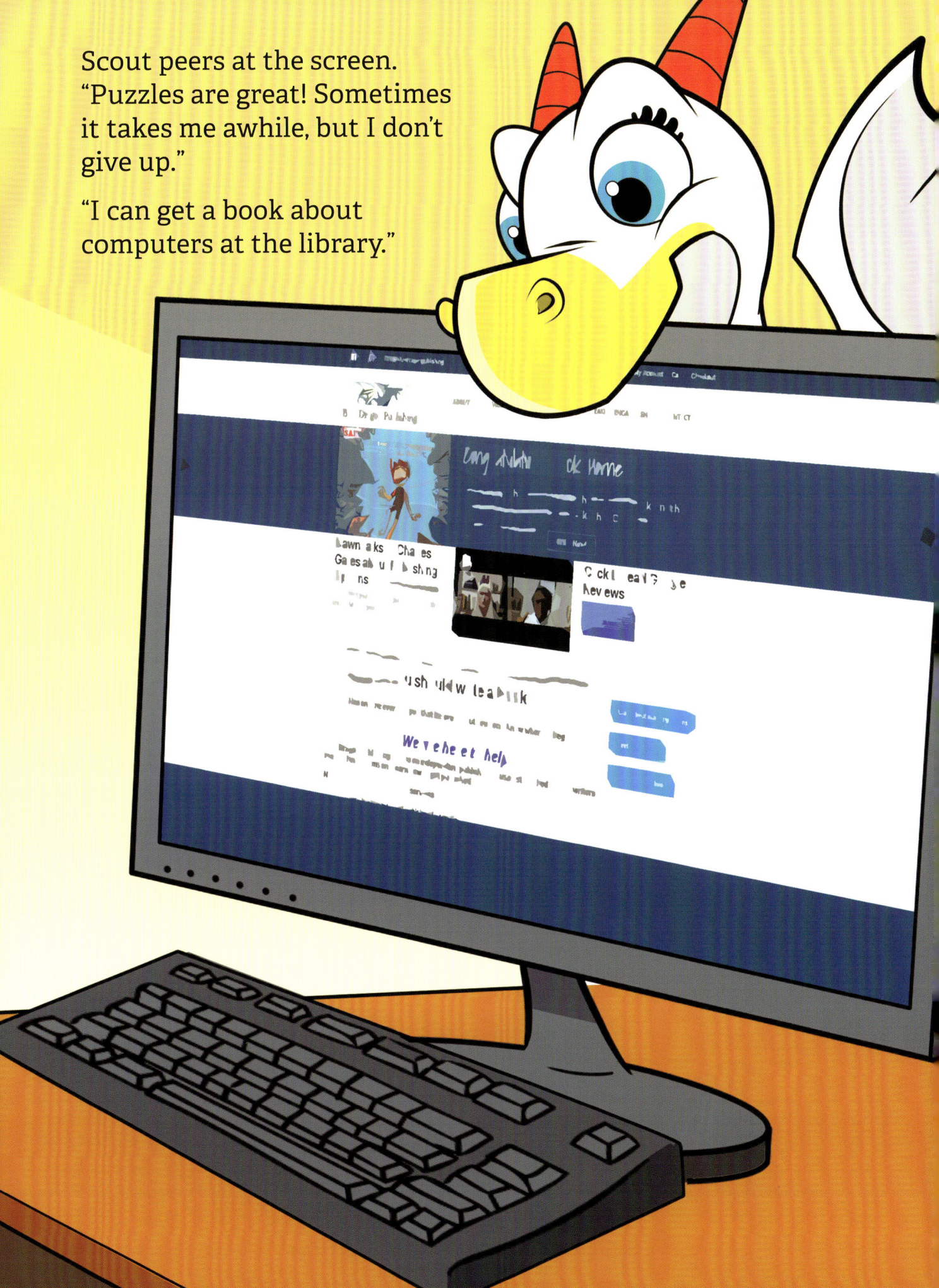

Scout peers at the screen. "Puzzles are great! Sometimes it takes me awhile, but I don't give up."

"I can get a book about computers at the library."

"If I look like you, I can be a **librarian**," Scout says.

"You don't have to look like me," says the librarian.

"Do you like tales of adventure? I find words wonderful! Nothing satisfies my hunger like a great story."

Scout selects a book. "I like adventure stories. My mom and I sit by the window and read together."

"Oh, look! There's someone outside *your* window."

"If I look like you, I can be a **window washer**," Scout says.

"You don't have to look like me," says the window washer.

"Do you enjoy making things sparkle? I polish the glass to let the sunshine in. I can see the whole city *and* lots of acorns from way up here."

Scout spies her reflection in the window. "One of my chores at home is dusting, and I'm not afraid of high places."

"Listen! The factory whistle is blowing!"

"If I look like you, I can be a **factory worker**," Scout says.

"You don't have to look like me," says the factory worker.

"Do you like putting things together? The click-clack of the machines is like music as I make things. All three of my hearts are happy when I'm working."

Scout watches the parts pass by on the belt. "Putting things together sounds like fun. But it's noisy in here. Maybe I should go outside."

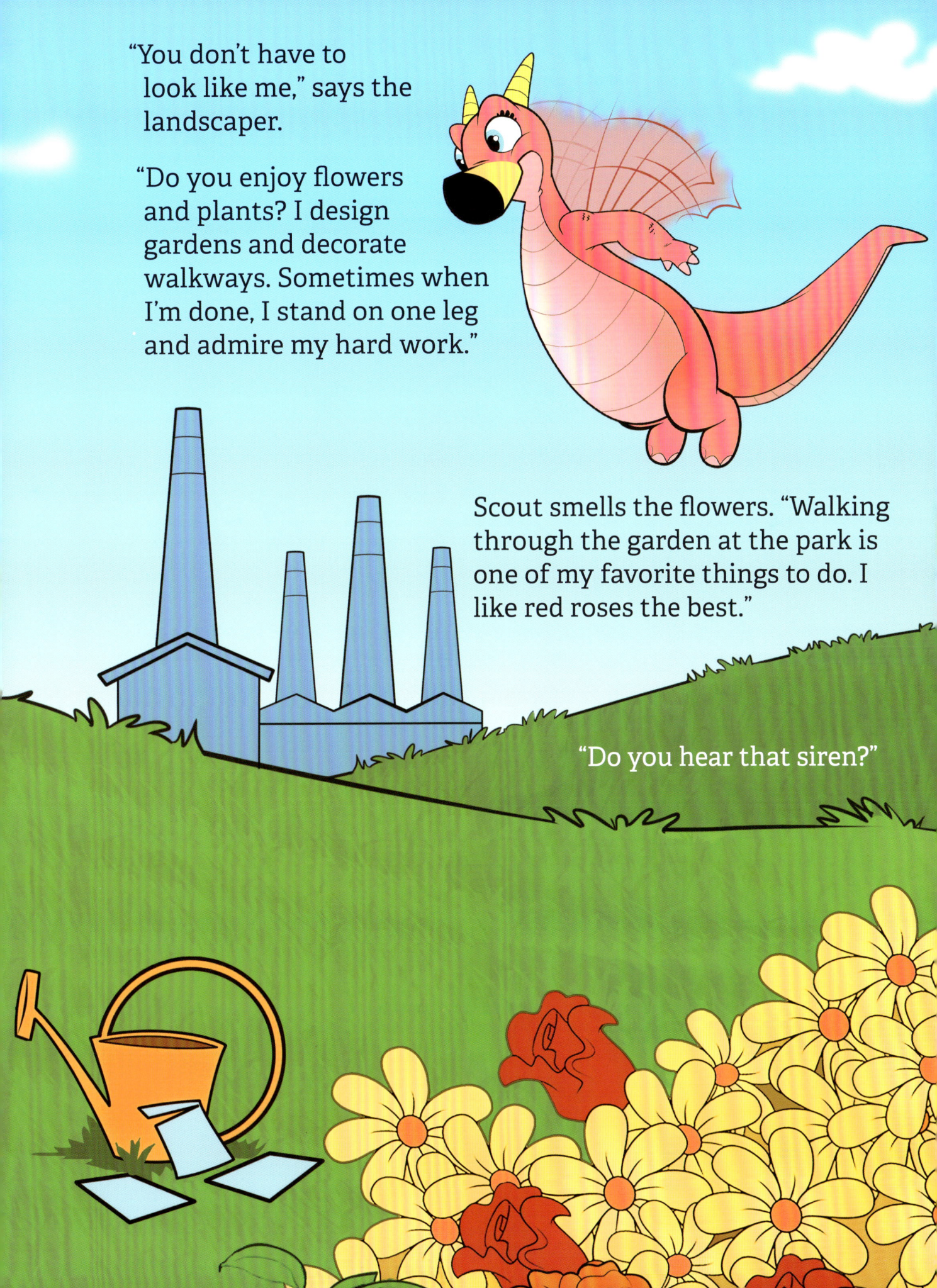
"You don't have to look like me," says the landscaper.

"Do you enjoy flowers and plants? I design gardens and decorate walkways. Sometimes when I'm done, I stand on one leg and admire my hard work."

Scout smells the flowers. "Walking through the garden at the park is one of my favorite things to do. I like red roses the best."

"Do you hear that siren?"

"If I look like you, I can be a **firefighter**," Scout says.

"You don't have to look like me," says the firefighter.

"Are you calm when others are scared? Working with my team to put out fires makes the load lighter. Speaking to students about safety is a special part of my job."

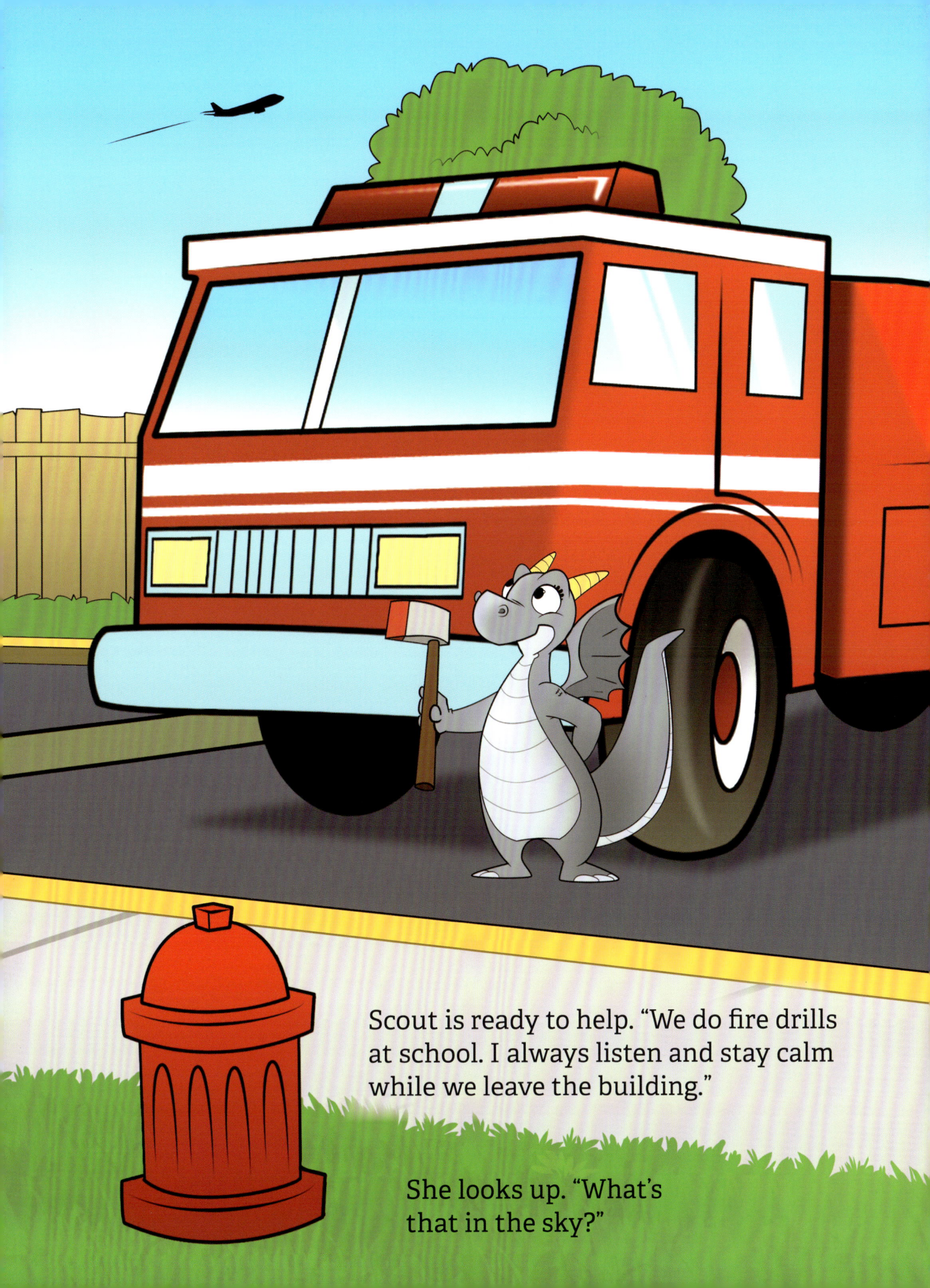

Scout is ready to help. "We do fire drills at school. I always listen and stay calm while we leave the building."

She looks up. "What's that in the sky?"

"If I look like you, I can be in the **Air Force**," Scout says.

"You don't have to look like me," says the airman.

"Do you like to travel and see new places? Flying airplanes is only part of what the Air Force does, and protecting our country is a privilege."

Scout stands proudly. "It's important to serve in the military, and flying is fun once you get used to the takeoff. But it's always nice to get home too."

"Momma, there are so many things I could be! It doesn't matter what I look like!"

"You're right, Scout," says her mother.

Scout thinks about her day. "I can't wait to explore more tomorrow."

What do you want to be?

About the Author

Dawn Brotherton is an award-winning author who draws on her experience as a colonel retired from the US Air Force as well as a softball coach and Girl Scout leader. Her variety of interests has led to a range of genres including picture books, middle grade sports, young adult fantasy, mystery, romance, and nonfiction.

She loves talking to people and visiting classrooms and Scout troops.

Dawn lives in Williamsburg, Virginia.

About the Illustrator

As a young boy, Chad's grandfather sat him down at the kitchen table and taught him how to draw cartoons. Chad never forgot those early lessons!

His love of drawing led him to the Columbus College of Art and Design. Upon graduation, he was hired by the Walt Disney Feature Animation studio in Florida. For the next seven years, he worked on animated movies such as Mulan, Lilo & Stitch, and Brother Bear.

Chad currently works as an illustrator and designer for a wide variety of clients. He continues to work in animation for smaller studios in Orlando.